The EarthBound Dreamer

Ella Ford

BookLeaf Publishing

Presentation by *BookLeaf Publishing*

Web: www.bookleafpub.com

E-mail: info@bookleafpub.com

ISBN: 9789395969819

First edition 2022

DEDICATION

I would like to dedicate this book to the empaths, the healers, those who regardless of hurt - choose to stay soft in a world that is not; your magic is important.

ACKNOWLEDGEMENT

I would like to acknowledge BookLeaf for giving me the opportunity to share my heart within these pages, thank-you.

To my beautiful older sisters Olivia and Hayleigh; thank-you for being my greatest teachers and bestfriends.

To my Dad, I love you, I miss you and I think about you often.

To my Mum, thank-you for gifting me this experience we call life; you are the strongest woman I know.

To my close friends, thank-you for believing in me and never leaving my side.

To those who have followed my journey and have supported and been excited for this book, thank-you.

I love you and thank god for you all.

PREFACE

This book was birthed by my experiences within the small part of the world I take up. I hope by reading my book, it opens up alternative doors and pathways within your own experience & judgement of your world. Art and poetry has been a big part of my healing journey, softening my edges, teaching me to be vulnerable, share and embrace the parts of myself that society is yet to see. Some days it's been my tears and screams running through the bristles of a brush and the scratches of a pen, other days it's been my love and compassion; but always my need for expression and self-exploration. Art and poetry give me the power to express what I have learnt through my life experiences & spiritual growth, and the opportunity to transform it in a way that allows me to share this knowledge, pain and triumphs with you all. I want realities and ways to be questioned, there's always room for growth. I grew up with witches holding wands and cauldrons, but the ability to share human experiences through rhyming words, pencils, pots of paint and brushes, now that's what I call magic. You're never alone, I love you and you are blessed to be "The EarthBound Dreamer."

The mind as it's tool

I've learnt Spirituality is a funny thing,
It's kind of like marriage to the entirety of yourself, minus a ring.
You learn to harmonise with parts of yourself and the world you didn't know existed;
Ego and soul no longer get twisted.
You learn that love and appreciation is the frequency of being,
But many don't know that because within themselves they are scared to go sightseeing.
What you see around you is merely a self reflection,
Realise that it's all just projection.
Fears and negativity are nothing but a game of the mind,
That's how the world tends to keep us blind.
Start by looking at what's right in front of you, not what's out of reach,
This along with gratitude is something that I will always preach.
What you want is right there,
and I say this without discarding any experiences of despair.
For if you take a moment to thank the universe for all it has given you,
Including the not so good days too.
The universe will see you appreciate life as it is both ups and downs;
and will have no choice but grant you grounds.

Because as I said earlier fear is a game of the mind,
but I failed to advise that there is more to this then you'll find;
For it is not restricted only to fear but most things throughout this lifetime.
Every feeling and moment is nothing until we make it into something in almost every situation,
So that tells us life truely exists within our mind and interpretations.
Practice staying neutral and this is a doing without suppressing the emotion,
But rather observing it without commotion.
Change your angle of observation,
and realise how you feel is only your creation.
We are human and will make mistake
but it's about what you learn from them, what you choose to take.
As you are granted with the choice to react not only outside but also within,
Master finding the good in everything and you will never not win.

My letter to love

The immense pain is where my seed was planted,
and the rain we shared together was when I no longer
took things for granted.
I was dedicated to being your umbrella and sun,
and it created ties that could never be undone.
My character development was strongly pushed by
our situation,
and through my silent pain,
self-love was the creation.
What I gained from our losses is so valuable,
even though for years personally things were
palpable.
The past you did not see
and scars that are metaphoric to a degree,
are what gave me the power to see,
that home wasn't only in you
but truly it was in me.
But just as I tell you what you didn't know,
even though it was all ages ago,
I thank you every day and have for the past 4 years,
forever I'm so grateful,
even for all the tears.
It's about time our love was due,
it feels like forever I've been so hungry for this
genuine love and I'm glad it's with you.
Now I have forever to signify to you the part of our
story you did not see,
the part that is such a big part of me.

I was so mad at the world for what it had done to you,
so much that I forgot to look after me too.
After so long of being a prisoner of night,
I got into meditation and began to build my own light.
Life without you became that little bit more trouble-free,
because of you I found love in me.
I began to put my belief in the Sky,
not in god,
but rather in space and time.
I believed eventually all would become aligned,
the universe decided to put me here and I spend my time writing a rhyme,
but not just for anyone but my twin flame of a lifetime.
Now being yours again it's as if I never belonged to any other,
it's obvious my soul has been in dormancy waiting for you to smother.
I always pulled through the stuff you never knew about,
and now I've learned to never hold onto doubt.
Spirit guides put you in my path and took you away,
to show me how to be independent for when we would meet again on a later day.
Though the heartbreak I learned that all I'll ever need is me,
and I needed that lesson so that together we could be in peace.
Even with an absent presence you continued to give me the most priceless gifts of all time,

and strangely as I've learnt and grown,
you once again are mine.
This just puts all my beliefs to reality,
and proves we have a love that goes beyond
mortality.
Reflecting on life I can see that not exactly you,
but still you within me,
gifted me so much including my spirituality.

Currency of eternal love

Angels are all around us in the very air we breathe -
Regularly he'd visit watching baby you teethe;
For souls know no concept of time,
He will spend his days gifting you courage to align.
Baby girl, even though I am gone,
My love for you is something that goes beyond.
For I now exist in the morning breeze;
And within your very veins baby girl, for you are my very own legacy.
Hear me in the leaves and feel me in the sun,
For baby girl life has just begun.
Let the rain remind you I'm never far;
For I also exist in up in the stars.
Even though I don't have eyes to see -
Energy is life's true currency.
I live in the sound of your laughter and the hand that wipes your tears away;
For baby girl, you are what I have to show for my best days.

Gone yet never forgotten

People would think I regularly stare into space,
But really I'm just daydreaming of your face.
Seeing the wrinkles of your eyes when you smile,
Makes all the pain worth it's while.
You live behind my eyes within the black space,
Yet of you when my eyes open there is no trace.
So I will sit in my silence and reminisce,
Because it is this version of you that I will always miss.

The unproductive heartbreak

Not interested in “self care” or candle lit baths,
This heartbreak will take another path.
Celebrating the small wins,
Like finally taking out overflowing bins.
Brushing days long untamed hair,
Being aware and conscious to not compare.
Cleaning up the mess of the mind,
In my room,
Smelling ever so slightly memories of you.
Trying to encourage myself to rearrange the items in this room,
So that when I open my door it’s no longer a stagnant energy tomb.
Finding an item of yours,
Triggered so many emotional detours.
Now I lay wet eyes and a heavy heart,
I might just sit and experience this part.
I’m not girl bossing this one out,
I’m learning what the opposite to that is all about.
Compassion for myself is what I need
If beyond the hustle I truely want to succeed.
I folded some clothes and put them away,
But I will give myself the break my heart is asking for and the rest I will leave for another day.

Mirrors, broken glass and silver spoons

When I look in the reflection it doesn't register as just what one can see,
it displays everything but what eyes see as "me."
Features tell a story but not one of life,
as it's rather a story that features could never truely begin to describe.
Although what is in the reflection is the beginning of any story,
yes that is true,
it doesn't answer the inquiry of the reflection which echos the daunting question of
"who really are you?"
If we are not our past then we are the choices we make,
the beginning of change, is the now along with the acceptance of mistake.
Choice is powerful as it is the equation,
it is the power and beginning of a manifestation.
Choice made can not be changed and so the ones chosen wrong will linger stained.
All that is left for one to do, is accept and move on,
but that is not without learning from the consequences the self brought upon.
So in the reflection of mirrors, broken glass and silver spoons,

I will stare a little longer,
and the understanding of choices one will reconquer.
With a fresh set of eyes and after hard lessons being learnt,
One can only go forward with this new understanding that choice can't ever be reversed.
This invitation of awareness and the power of now,
is a realisation that I am and always have been only what I will allow.
The amazing thing of choice is that it goes hand in hand with a constant opportunity for change,
And so the registration of reflection can always be rearranged.
And so when I ask myself "who are you?"
I'll answer that because it's whatever in the reflection of mirrors, broken glass or silver spoons, with this new awareness, I chose to do.

Only human

I winced, I am only human
You replied - I don’t want an excuse.
But only human, is everyone’s truth.

Inner-healing

I'm learning to fight my battles not with fists nor swords,
But rather with beautiful music and quiet prayers behind closed doors.

I love you

It doesn't matter how flawed you believe you are,
The right people will stick around.
And those who leave
Are creating space
For those who will love you so much harder.

Family

We shall always forgive, love and grow, for this
is our parents first time on this Earth too.
~ learning never stops

The lonely girls lullaby

People come and go,
Let them.
Thank their contribution to your life, they helped shape you.
Because of them, you're one step closer to who you're meant to be.
Do not beg.
Do not chase.
Because for them there is no longer a place.
Do not fret or sit in hate,
For it's your choice with their absence, what you want to create.
Remember like all emotions, they're only a phase;
Realise that god truely does work in mysterious ways.
On your own, sit with your tears, you'll be okay.
Just do not beg someone who doesn't see your worth to stay.
I'm talking to you like an older sister, yes I know;
But I just want to see you reach your potential, see you grow.
These tears will water your soul,
and in no time you will realise on your own,
you are whole.

Tangerine Dream

I just want to be your girl dressed pretty and in white,
But I see I am not in white,
Rather a tangerine dream.
That you can binge on like sweet cuisine.
Do you see me with flowers in my hair?
Is this garden within your ability to repair?
My stem is curved, shoulders are slumped,
But all that can be seen is me being blunt.
I am not in white,
But better yet, I am a tangerine dream.
I pray you have an ache in your sweet tooth,
Because my sugar awaits your esteem.

To be held

Was I too much when your fingers were in my
mouth?
Was I too much when they traced my body south?
Or was I only too much when tears rolled on my
cheeks?
What if I told you it was because I had been feeling
unloved for weeks?
Instead of holding me or kissing my forehead,
You told me you felt uncomfortable in your own bed.
Although times have been rough,
I was only too much, because your space for me,
wasn't enough.

You can say no.

There will be a time you say no,
And everything you've done in their life,
in their mind will go,
But comfort yourself and let yourself know,
You can't please everyone, you can say no.
You deserve more than seasonal changing love,
you are allowed say no and supporting you is the lord above.
Let go of saving face,
Listen to your thoughts, and in your heart have faith.

Star seedling

Do not go abandoning who you are because they did,
you are more than the love another human has or
doesn't have for the light you are.

The loudest silence

Everytime the phone rings I am hoping it's you
I just want to know if you still think about me too.
My heart feels so heavy, is your love language still gooey and sappy?
Now I stare out of my window and wonder who you'll marry.
Am I selfish for missing you although it was me who let go?
Now I have no choice but to go with the flow.
I despise of god at times,
but I know it's all apart of his sacred designs.
What is next?
Am I to know?
All that I know, is I can't put a pause on what I am destined to outgrow.
Time is writing my lines,
But I am here to pay the fines.
To be head strong makes my heart weak,
God please I pray that things don't become oblique.
Now when my phone rings, I know it's not you,
Yet I still hope once in a while you think of me, like I think of you too.
I still see you in the moon and stars,
as what you made me feel, forever claimed the sky as ours.

You are forever

During the human experience, we forget, or are yet to be taught that beyond the ego, we are eternal beings.

Do you see me?

The connection between skin brings a comfort to an aching soul as it is a temporary pain relief to the loneliness we tend to disguise as "love."

The moons whisper

I apologise for stripping you of all that you've
known.
But use me as an example, for in all my phases, I still
glow.
My plan has more in store for you, so I will remove
what you have outgrown.
There is still so much more in this life for you to be
shown.
I'm teaching you the art of letting go,
so let go,
Because no longer can your growth can be
postponed.

The apology you deserved

I apologise for stripping you and leaving you bare.
Your hand was the only warmth my heart knew,
and being without it felt unfair.
I'm sorry I robbed you of your worth when you no longer were of use to me,
It was really hard to see a life without us being "we."
I promise you it came from a place of love,
I'm sorry I took my hurt out on you instead of praying to what is above.
I thought it would be easier to see you as someone you're not,
But through my hurt, the promises I made for your safety, I forgot.
I couldn't accept that you're doing what you feel is right for you,
It felt unfair that it didn't include me too.
Now that we are apart I can see you did what was best not only for you, but for us.
So I pray for your happiness and i realise your love wasn't everything,
it was a plus.
So I'm sorry, I love you and I forgive you.
May you be sorry, love me and forgive me one day too.
In your own time, from a distance, wherever you are,
May your heart heal from our scar.

Romanticise your Life

Our souls crave intimacy
Community, passion,
So why with our love do we ration?
Beneath it all we truely want to feel and love so much that it bleeds beyond our being,
Because it is that state that is the most freeing.
Not within money, status or power,
But rather to treat ourselves and life like a delicate flower.
Only then will we feel the most alive,
If within ourselves and eachother we no longer fear the deepest of dives.

www.ingramcontent.com/pod-product-compliance
Lightning Source LLC
Chambersburg PA
CBHW051755130826
49812CB00033B/1164